Behind Closed Doors

A Collection of Unusual Poetry

By Robbie Cheadle

Compiled and Edited by

Kaye Lynne Booth

Photography and fondant illustrations by Robbie Cheadle

Cover design by Teagan R. Geneviene

About this book, Behind Closed Doors

As with many other areas in life, my thoughts about poetry seem to differ from many other people. When I write poetry, which isn't that often compared to the time I spend writing prose, it is usually an explosion of thoughts and/or emotions. The whole poem comes into my mind fully formed. I don't struggle for words or ideas and I don't usually do a huge amount of editing outside of looking for word echoes, improving word choices, and eliminating words that hinder the rhythmic flow of the poem. I never sit down and deliberately try to write a poem.

My poems are either expressions of joy or celebrations of relationships and events or they are criticisms of situations that I perceive as unjust or inequitable in some way.

This volume of poems includes several limericks I wrote during lockdown. These limericks, together with a cake art illustration relevant to the point being made, strike at the heart of certain social issues that arose during lockdown and that rankled with me.

I have moved my cake art in the direction of making cakes that make a social statement about environmental and other issues. The Covid-19 cakes are examples of this artwork, as are the two cakes that illustrate the twisted nursery rhymes included in this book.

I hope you enjoy this unusual collection of poems and appreciate some of the deeper meanings behind the limericks, twisted nursery rhymes, and cake art.

In the boardroom

Masks

(tanka poems)

What thoughts are hidden

Behind her immobile face

Quite expressionless

Eyes cold and indifferent

Scrutinising me – hawk like

***

I've many faces

And ways of innovating

Vision unleashed

It flies with gossamer wings

My world multi-faceted

Opportunity

(tanka poem)

Make your own success

Leave no pathway untrodden

Opportunity

Will knock only once in life

Be sure to answer the door

Trust

(tanka poems)

Always remember

When studying the outside

Of anything in life

That it may be misleading

And tell agreeable lies

***

Can you trust your eyes?

Really believe what they see?

Or is it only

An illusion or cheap trick

Behind which the truth loiters?

Hope

(tanka poem)

Eyes jaded by life

Suddenly experience

Renewal of shine

When life's path makes a U-turn

Leading back towards the light

Achieving tranquillity

Tranquillity

A state of calm

Or peacefulness

That is achieved,

I've been told,

By quietening the mind

And composing the spirit

To me, it's reality

Is a shrivelled seed

That's failed to thrive

Due to lack of care

And nurturing

For many a year

I've spent my life

Yoyoing between

Chaotic panic

And lesser anxiety

Never reaching

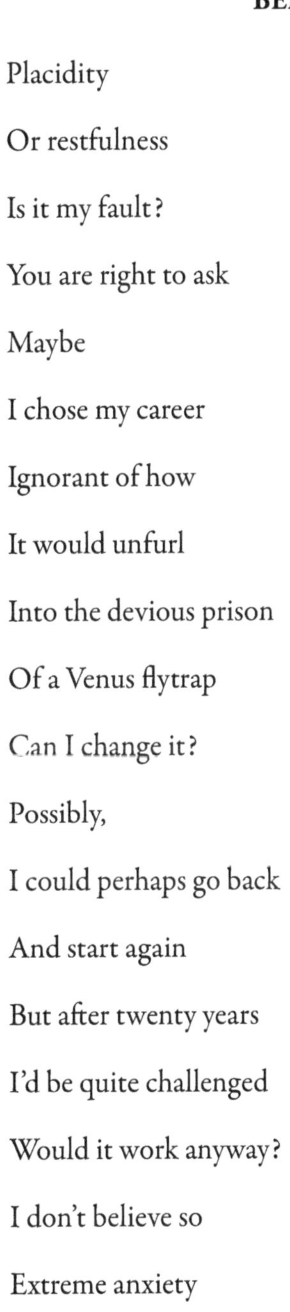

Placidity

Or restfulness

Is it my fault?

You are right to ask

Maybe

I chose my career

Ignorant of how

It would unfurl

Into the devious prison

Of a Venus flytrap

Can I change it?

Possibly,

I could perhaps go back

And start again

But after twenty years

I'd be quite challenged

Would it work anyway?

I don't believe so

Extreme anxiety

Now so embedded

Into my work ethos

It has become

My deviant way of life

Living on the edge

Fuelled by adrenaline

Pressured to deliver

Ignoring personal cost

Lured by success

And money

Too much time has passed

Such behaviour

Too ingrained

To be easily amended

I may go to my grave

Without ever experiencing

Tranquillity

Experience

(tanka poems)

My experience

Demonstrates no black or white

Only shades of grey

That can be interpreted

In the manner we see fit

***

Spread your wings and fly

But when the going gets tough

Be adaptable

Glide sideways or upside down

If it helps achieve your goals

Do you want it enough?

You tell me you want

Your time in the sun

To dance in the light

That reflects off your fame

Do you really want it?

Do you crave it enough?

To give up the good things

Like relaxation and rest

Sleeping late in your bed

Toasty and warm

Are you sufficiently mesmerised

By the task to hand

To trade pleasure for work?

And sit in your office,

Juggling ideas and possibilities,

While your friends watch movies,

Eat out, drink, and socialise

Spending their weekends

Having a jolly good time

Can you be disciplined and sit

At a computer for hours

Tapping out words

While creating settings

Actions and events

That form themselves into stories?

Will you watch

The world passing by

Through the glass of your window?

While you pursue the fantasy

You hope to achieve,

Knowing there are no guarantees

Few things in this life

Come without paying a price

And the tag accompanying fame

And its bedfellow fortune

Is always high

Taxing time and good health

With no assured return

Are you ready to exchange

Your freedom and pleasure

For the discipline required

To chase that elusive light?

The corporate hunt

An external threat

Is hard to overcome

The hunter pitilessly

And relentlessly pursuing

A defenceless prey

Ultimately ravaging

The unwary target

Ending its life

Without remorse

It then moves on

Without a backward glance

Not taking the time

To feed from its kill

'Though if it's convenient

Well-aimed blows

Continue to rain down

Indiscriminately

on the prostrate body

It helps to believe
That the inner circle
Will rally around
To defend its own
The horror mounts
When trust is broken
Colleagues turning
On one another
Ruthlessly savaging
Those who've displayed
Loyalty and trust
There are no friendships
In the corporate jungle
Colleagues left to demise
In this uncaring world

Making a splash

How do you see

Your life unfolding?

What gives you purpose?

What inspires you

To get up each morning

And face the day?

Do you care

If your actions

Leave the surface

Of your life

And that of others

Smooth and unmarred?

Or is it your ambition

To create ripples

Across its glassy face?

Do you think it's vital

To make an impact

Doing or saying something

That is noteworthy

Possibly inspiring change

That benefits us all

What is your purpose?

To leave an untroubled surface

Or to make a big splash

Climbing the corporate ladder

(tanka poems)

From the hot ashes

Of a destructive burning

A phoenix will rise

On golden wings of passion

New challenges must be faced

***

Desire for greatness

To see their name in bright lights

And make a big splash

Is what drives overachievers

To push the outer limits

After death

Death's finality

(tanka prose)

Desperately, she peers through the dimness. An assorted array of items drift past her: crockery, bed linen, even a violin. She can't see what she's looking for. She keeps moving forward. It must be here somewhere.

Her long nightdress clings to her legs, slowing her forward motion. An elderly couple float past her. They are dressed in their best finery. The bright red of the gentleman's bow tie is startling against his black dress suit. Their eyes are closed as if in sleep.

She catches a glimpse of it out of the corner of her eye. She reaches out and wraps her small, white fingers around the wooden doll. Her treasured possession in her grasp she drifts towards the Nether Gate. The other victims of the shipwreck were already being sucked through.

How final is death?

What loiters beyond the veil?

I would love to know

Have certainty, without doubt

Instead, I will just believe

Thoughts

(tanka poems)

Introspective thoughts

Can plunge your soul into Hell

Inward focus lets

Misguided ideas rule

Leaving emptiness behind

***

Distantly you hear

The faint notes of a swan song

As the clock ticks on

Thoughts and memories erode

The end coming rapidly

***

When death comes calling

Reaching out his gentle hand

Our pain is intense

Watching a dear one depart

Hardest for those left behind.

***

From the first moment

We breath the air of this world

Our death draws nearer

Some go early and some late

But we all walk the same path

In my mind

A fabricated world

Is our modern world

a complete fabrication

where nothing is true

and our lives are woven

into a fabric of deception?

Our food looks appealing

its presentation tasty and appetizing

the plastic packaging sealing in

its artificial nutrition and goodness

But it lacks real sustenance

and carries the potential

to seal our physical doom

carcinogenics thriving and alive

in its well-preserved perfection

hidden carefully among

its enhanced colours and flavours

Our homes are not robust

do not allow us the privileged
of privacy and solitude
filled as they are with
the instruments of spies
Hidden cameras and microphones
are attached to each gadget
like prefabricated buildings
that share every secret
through their insubstantial walls
Our politicians feed us half-truths
even blatant lies are acceptable
as they twist events and circumstances
into the perfect lifestyle fable
nothing considered sacred or holy
at the altar of greed and power
If I had a reasonable alternative
I would turn away from it all
and place my faith at the door
of my own impossible fantasy
of an old-fashioned lifestyle

Perspective

(tanka poems)

Is it possible

To escape conformity

And break your shackles

By riding a bicycle

With your face into the wind?

***

During times of trial

A different perspective

Is required by all

In order to innovate

Reaching the improbable

Can you see the butterflies?

Can you see the butterflies?

Bright splashes of vibrancy

daubs of colour

against an azure sky.

Can you see the butterflies?

On near transparent wings

they flutter and fly

deliciously light on the breeze.

Can you see the butterflies?

A cloud of beauty

acting as one

a gossamer pool of delight.

I can see the butterflies

through half closed eyes

my dreams form shapes

with fluttering wings.

I can see the butterflies

as they develop in my mind

elusive thoughts grow wings

and they fly.

In the dark

The sun's sliding downward in the West
The cold, a most unwelcome guest
When it's time to put on heaters and lights
That's when load shedding really bites.

Life is tough at the best of times
Bittersweet, a bit like limes
It stretches most people to the hilt
Without extra things to make life tilt.

It's difficult, trying to get things done
Cooking in the dark is not much fun
It's even worse getting kids to study
Any excuse to stop and chat to a buddy.

We are blessed; we have gas and a genie*
Although this costs a pretty penny
We are better off than the rest
Of the situation we should make the best.

So why then do I feel so bad
No traffic lights make me mad

When I lie in the dark at night

Every noise I hear gives me a fright.

Maybe the oversees pastures really are greener

Even if our life may be a bit leaner

At least the lights will reliably work

And lack of power won't drive me berserk.

*Colloquial term for a generator

Sleep

(tanka poem)

Gratefully she sinks

Into sleep's loving embrace

Thoughts gently unfurl

Reorganising themselves

Answers revealed in sweet dreams

Stars in her eyes

A dreamer
she was born
with stars in her eyes

They enabled her
allowing escape
from the routine
of her daily life

She would look up
and imagine herself
far, far way
sailing on a ship
across a wide blue sea
diving for pearls
in a hidden cove
weaving shells
into her golden hair
while singing a duet
with a friendly mermaid

The dreary task at hand
left behind, undone
as she danced, unfettered
in her own, glittering world

The stars gave her hope
allowed her to soar
on the gossamer wings
of an unencumbered mind
saving her from drowning
in a sea of black despair

Those strange stars
empowered her
giving her the tools
to write and create
stories for others
to read and enjoy

One day, when those eyes
close for the last time
a bit of fairy dust
from her starry eyes

will stay behind

forever

Behaviour

(haiku poems)

Standing united

Against the scourge of deceit

Ignites flames of hope

***

Dark clouds surround me

As I attempt to break free

Guided by the light

Behaviour

(tanka poems)

Will pointless goading
Have a negative impact
On your daily life?
Will summonsing interest
From dark angels seal your fate

***

Experience life
Seize the opportunities
Face your challenges
Do not hide in the shadows
You control your destiny

Reactions

(tanka poems)

We create our luck

Through hard work and industry

Destiny's impact

May require interventions

But that is controllable

***

When you are hurting

And nursing your many wounds

Don't turn life away

Healing is much easier

When pursuing a challenge

In the home

Contrasting colours

(a metaphorical poem)

My husband is....	I am....
a calm expanse of water; glass smooth and clear,	a whirlpool of relentless, swirling motion,
a gentle zephyr, mildly puffing through life,	a tornado, tearing across fields and dales,
a leader with a firm attitude and commanding tone,	a soldier, determinedly marching through life,
a tawny owl, silent, watchful and wise,	a red breasted robin; bright eyed, perky and daring,
a spacious cavern, silent, restful and still,	a babbling stream; vibrant, noisy and turbulent,
a grandfather clock, steadily marking the seconds, minutes, and hours,	a cuckoo clock that loudly announces the hour,
a dictionary, providing an exact and definitive meaning,	a mysterious poem with different shades of meaning,
a mighty redwood, solid, sturdy and dependable,	a daylily flowering in a myriad of deep and bright colours,
a mural painted in calming blues and greens,	a collage of bright colours; yellows, oranges and pinks.
classic piano; gently soothing, relaxing, and soft,	raucous Broadway tunes; loud, lusty, and energised.

Our hero

Our hero, he stands

So tall and strong

It is reassuring to know

It's to him we belong

Clever and confident

Yet quick with a smile

Always willing and able

To go that extra mile

With his sons he will play

A practice cricket match

Then inside he'll give a hand

A rat with glue will catch

Generous with money

Almost to a fault

Not superstitious though

Don't throw spilt salt

But beware of obtaining his agreement

To renovations or a damp proofing cure

He'll never change his mind again

So, you'd better be quite sure

He walks away

From the first day

he took a tentative step

on uncertain chubby legs

attached to adventurous feet

he moved away from her

embracing with enthusiasm

the mysterious outside world

She watched over him tenderly

as he learned about life

discovered the joy of friendship

and the heartbreak of loss

embarked on his academic journey

exploiting his strengths and

overcoming his weaknesses

and during all this time

mom was always enough

her smile healed all wounds

her kiss cured all pain

but she knew in her heart
that this investment of hers
was ultimately for another
a nameless faceless other
who would eventually take her place
she was preparing him to leave
and find his place in this world

His independence draws ever closer
her smile no longer enough
as he jostles for position
in the heartless world of men
her kiss no longer wanted
as he seeks the lips of the other

It's heart wrenching to let go
knowing he must suffer pain
before he finds his enduring love
encounter setbacks and loss
before success and satisfaction
but it's the duty of a mother
to set her son loose

to fly alone

Our Mother

There she sits, small, and yet so tough

Always ready to tell us when enough is enough

Our number one fan when things go well

Always there to help us up, when down we fell

Her home cooked meals are a delightful thought

As are the important messages which she taught

The best ways to get a cake to rise

Never to tell our friends or family lies

How to eat nicely with a fork and knife

How a little kindness goes a long way in life

Amazing mom, we are blessed to have you near

As you are the person, we hold most dear

My Sunshine

I love my little Sunshine

He is the sweetest boy

I often give him cuddles

And buy him a nice new toy

We read our favourite stories

About dragons and brave knights

He thoroughly enjoys them

Then out go all the lights

From closed cupboards and doors

Lurking monsters stealthily creep

And my poor little lad

Can't get a wink of sleep

Into the marital bed

My son quietly slides

And between his loving parents

Form night-time horrors hides

Mom and Dad lie awake

While their son kicks and dreams

Unable to get any shuteye

Counting sheep won't work, it seems

Reactions

(haiku poems)

When you have children

Your heart will forever beat

Outside your body

***

One person must lead

And be positioned above

All the rest of us

A fairy-tale come true

(a metaphorical poem)

A wedding is....

a cascading backdrop of white
roses, green foliage and lights,

a splash of happiness along the
path of life,

a babble of good cheer and
enthusiasm,

a beautiful bride, swathed in fine
lace, tulle and silk,

a gathering of groomsman – full of
vigour and energy,

a gaggle of bridesmaids – giggling
in cream,

an orchestra of sound - soft music,
laughter and tears,

a dreamy occasion, full of mystery
and delight,

an opportunity to celebrate, dress
up and have fun,

a solemn event, when two lives
merge and become one,

a celebration of Faith, God's
wisdom and goodness,

a mosaic of loved ones forming a
pattern of support,

a miraculous joining of two hearts
and two souls,

a passionate sermon, that amazes
and uplifts,

parents of the bride, keeping a
daughter – gaining a son,

a melting pot of family and friends -
all backgrounds and ages,

a testimony of love from
grandparents and parents,

the meaning of it all – our very
reason for being.

Wedding fun

Down the aisle she floats

Complexion, peaches 'n cream

Hair, a spun gold mass
Shimmering in a bright sunbeam

Dress a gorgeous creation
Shoes and veil, match
A playful zephyr blows
The veil on a twig to catch

Her happiness, like sunshine
Is a joy to behold
Their love is a journey
Just starting to unfold

The groom, strong and manly
Full of fun and smiles
Easily he ensnared her
With his attentive wiles

The guests gaze enchanted
As they take their vows
The bride, blushes and giggles
He, his audience, wows

We wish them all the best
As they start their life together

Their bonds of love strong

To last from now, forever

We love you, Daddy

Daddy, you must know
You're our number one guy
When we're right down low
And when we're flying high

As tiny mites you tickled us
Which made us laugh and giggle
Told long family anecdotes
Which made us yawn and wriggle

You taught us to look after things
And made us clean our bikes
Polishing spokes 'til they shone
Still, something none of us likes

You are our first port of call
When things are going badly
Your help we all appreciate
Most gratefully and gladly

Our sister into labour went
While travelling in her car

You are the one she called

To come rushing from afar

As we travel our chosen path

Men will come and leave

But you will always be the best

We honestly believe

During lockdown

Lockdown in poverty

(limericks)

Poverty makes stockpiling a farce

In some places, it can't come to pass

Nothing spare, money's tight

Sickness, an everyday fight

Everything needed is always sparse

***

If we're sick, we're supposed to isolate

Not a concept to which the poor can relate

When you live in a tin roofed shack

And water and basic amenities you lack

An out-of-control virus will just devastate

No contact

(tanka poem)

My life feels ghostlike

Insubstantial and unreal

No human contact

No office; only on-line

Nothing left to keep me here

Highs and Lows

(haibun)

Lifting her eyes, she gazed out of the window at the garden. The sun shone, flowers bloomed, and birds sang. The cycle of life continued all around her as she sat there, struggling to work on this lovely afternoon.

This pandemic's a strange situation, she thought.

Some people have been pulled into a cycle of endless work, trying to save businesses from demise through capital and debt raisings. Others sit at home, on furlough or unemployed, wishing they were at work.

Over the past year, her work deadlines had become shorter and shorter, as businesses struggled for survival in a locked down world. They needed their cash or debt lifelines yesterday and that put huge pressure on debt restructuring and corporate finance employees to deliver.

All respect for working hours had disappeared. Her team had been working twelve to fourteen-hour days for months, and some ended up working through the night a few times a week. They'd worked every weekend for nine weeks in a row. There were no breaks between Zoom meetings which were set up back-to-back all day long. Exercise, coffee, and lunch breaks, and even late evening relaxation had been dispensed with. An expectation of availability at all hours of the day and night was the new normal.

After all, if you are stuck at home all day and night, why shouldn't you work all the time? It's not like you have anything else to do.

Everyone focused on the frontline workers and gave them accolades, which they did undoubtedly deserve. But few people even knew about the millions of people working tirelessly to save the economy and prevent a complete implosion of our modern lifestyles.

How long can we continue like this, on a Ferris wheel of anxiety, going around and around in a static setting?

Her life is spinning

Highs and lows like a Ferris wheel

Are achieved daily.

Other Worldly

My life has become
quite surreal
other worldly
One day I had freedom
the next, it was gone.

How will this end?
I find myself wondering
Will we take a big step
backwards in time
fifty years or more?

Will single income households
become the norm of our lives?
Our holidays spent at home
tidying out cupboards
and spring cleaning the house?
Will a day trip to the beach
be the ultimate family treat?

Or will we take a leap forward

into the Fourth Industrial Revolution?

Will we shop on digital platforms

without moving from our couches?

Order our children from a lab

with a genetic ideal request form?

Have our DNA sliced and diced

to prevent dreaded disease?

All except this one

which has shattered our world?

It all seems so very

other worldly.

Inevitable side-effects of Zoom and working from home

(limericks)

He sat on his cellular phone in the room

Having just finished a meeting on Zoom

What a frightening sight

His expression, dark as night

The seed of a monster starting to bloom

Endless back-to-back meetings on Zoom

Fill employees with a sense of gloom

The leader strikes like a snake

When colleagues make a mistake

When will it end and normality resume?

***

Staring at a cell phone screen all day

Instead of going out to run and play

Turns eyes vacant and round

The lack of energy is profound

Their way of life has gone astray

Lockdown days

During lockdown we're forced

to spend time at home

gone all possibility

of spending time alone

The room we always used

to sit down and eat

Is covered in schoolbooks

And far from being neat.

I've discovered new attributes

my husband kept concealed

his grizzly bear side

has now been revealed.

Who would have thought

a teacher I'd become

to ensure my boys years of learning

do not quickly come undone.

The pain in my back

is now here to stay

my physiotherapy's been postponed

to another distant day.

From my OCD son

I've had to hide the soap

even the old fashioned one

that hangs from a rope.

His anxiety about sickness

has reached an all-time high

he seeks reassurance I can't give

without telling him a lie.

We are all in this together

all in the same proverbial boat

remember that when you're grumpy

we all need to keep going and afloat.

Children are Coronavirus vectors

(limericks)

"Stay away!" the witch did yell

I'm already feeling most unwell

Hand sanitizer didn't work

My keep-well spell had a quirk

Now I've no sense of smell

Hansel and Gretel could quickly tell

The witch was not feeling well

She kept herself hidden away

With a mask and hand spray

Covid-19 impervious to her spell

In nature

The crimson rose

The crimson rose

Stands tall and alone

A stately queen

On a deep green throne

Surrounded by guards

Thorns barbed and fierce

Unsuspecting fingers

They harshly pierce

Each delicate petal

With a texture of velvet

Such stately splendour

We surely must covet

What secret thoughts

Does this artistry invoke

What wicked actions

Such mystery must revoke

Its cloying fragrance

Permeates each breath

Bringing to mind thoughts

Of peaceful death

I saw a fish a-swimming

(twisted nursery rhyme)

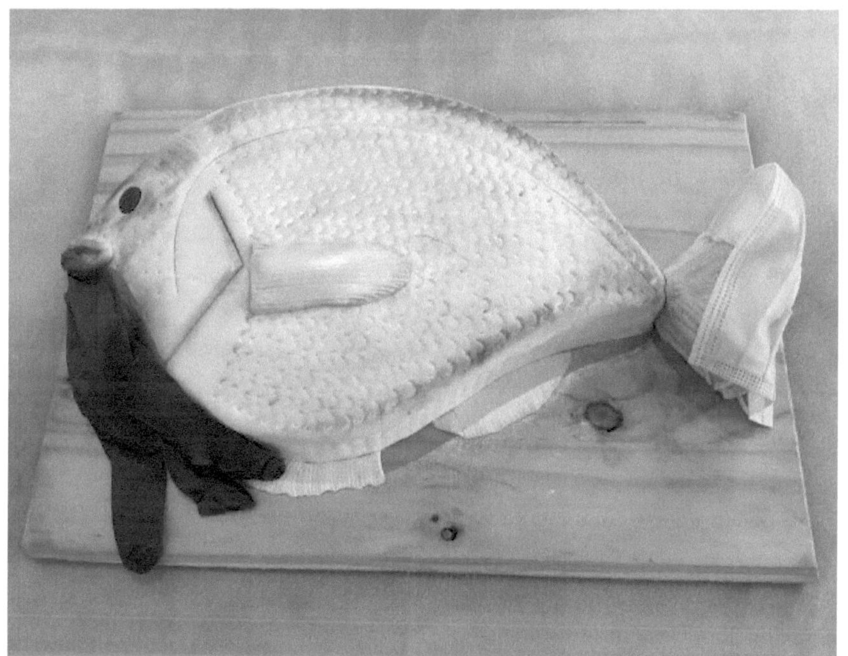

I saw a fish a-swimming

A-swimming in the sea

Both fins were badly mangled

Its eyes held a desperate plea

In a mask it was entangled

Gills smothered by a fold

If help was not forthcoming

It would soon be dead and cold

An ocean filled with medical masks

Is not what the fish expect

If mankind doesn't change its behaviour

Who knows what will be extinct next

Plastic gloves fill up their stomachs

When they swallow what looks like a snack

They die a grim death from starvation

Because of the discipline people lack

The river

(haiku poems)

Water like satin

Reflecting the clear blue sky

Hiding deadly threats

***

A smug crocodile

Seeking an easy dinner

Foiled by angry mom

***

The frothy white wake

Flows behind the speeding boat

Disturbing nature

The best gift of all

I woke up on Christmas morning

And what miracle did I hear?

The splatter of heavy rainfall

It's sound so distinctive and clear

Santa, I'm glad you got my wish list

And thought my request worthwhile

The downpour has revived the earth

The flowers are sparkling in style

Water, in Africa, a most precious gift

I wonder, were the clouds in your sack?

Your gift to South Africa and its people

Will help alleviate a serious lack

If the polar icecaps doth melt

(based on the North wind doth blow)

If the polar icecaps doth melt

And global warming makes itself felt

What will the earth look like then?

Poor thing.

Some areas will be dry

The plant life will wilt and die

And not a single bird will sing

Poor thing.

About Robbie Cheadle

Robbie Cheadle is a children's author and poet.

The Sir Chocolate children's picture books, co-authored by Robbie and Michael Cheadle, are written in sweet, short rhymes which are easy for young children to follow and are illustrated with pictures of delicious cakes and cake decorations. Each book also includes simple recipes or biscuit art directions which children can make under adult supervision.

Robbie has also published books for older children which incorporate recipes that are relevant to the storylines.

Robbie writes a monthly series for https://writingtoberead.com called "Growing Bookworms". This series discusses different topics relating to the benefits of reading to children.

Robbie has a blog, https://robbiesinspiration.wordpress.com/ where she shares book reviews, recipes, author interviews, and poetry.

Robbie also publishes books for adults under the name Roberta Eaton Cheadle.

Poetry Books by Robbie Cheadle

Open a new door (co-written with Kim Blades)

Open a New Door is a poetic peep into the lives of the poets, Kim Blades and Robbie Cheadle, both of whom live in South Africa.

The book is divided into four categories: God bless Africa, God bless my family and friends, God bless me, and God bless corporates and work. Each part is sub-divided into the good, the bad and the ugly of the two poets' experiences, presented in rhyming verse, free-style, haiku and tanka, in each of these categories and include colourful depictions of their thoughts and emotions.

The purpose of this book of poetry is encapsulated in the following tanka and haiku poems:

What drives me to write?

To share my innermost thoughts

The answer is clear

It's my personal attempt

To make some sense of this world.

Inspiration blossoms

Like the unfurling petals

Of the Desert Rose

Poetry anthology including poems by Roberta Eaton Cheadle

Poetry Treasures

Poetry Treasures is a collection of poetry from the poet/author guests of Robbie Cheadle on the "Treasuring Poetry" blog series on Writing to be Read in 2020. Open the book and discover the poetry treasures of Sue Vincent, Geoff Le Pard, Frank Prem, Victoria (Tori) Zigler, Colleen M. Chesebro, K. Morris, Annette Rochelle Aben, Jude Kirya Itakali, and Roberta Eaton Cheadle.

Thank You for Reading

Behind Closed Doors.

Reviews are Hugs
For Authors.
Hug your Authors!

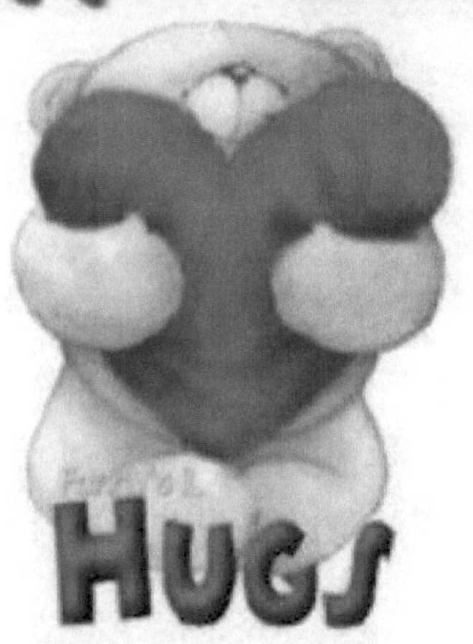

If you Enjoyed this Poetry Collection, be sure to leave a review and support the Poet/author.

Visit the *WordCrafter* website and social media pages,

and the *Writing to be Read* authors' blog:

WordCrafter Website: https://kayebooth.wixsite.com/wordcrafter

Facebook: https://www.facebook.com/WordCrafterServices/

LinkedIn: https://www.linkedin.com/company/wordcrafter-enterprises/?viewAsMember=true

Writing to be Read: http://writingtoberead.com

About the Publisher

WordCrafter Press publishes quality books and anthologies. Learn more about *WordCrafter* and keep updated on current online book events, writing contests, up coming book blog tours and new releases on the *Writing to be Read* authors' blog: https://writingtoberead.com/

www.ingramcontent.com/pod-product-compliance
Ingram Content Group UK Ltd.
Pitfield, Milton Keynes, MK11 3LW, UK
UKHW041822200726
13854UKWH00001BA/440

9 798201 758264